Dancing in the Rain

Mzi Mahola

⎡U⎤
KZN
PRESS UNIVERSITY OF KWAZULU-NATAL PRESS

Published in 2006 by University of KwaZulu-Natal Press
Private Bag X01
Scottsville 3209
South Africa
Email: books@ukzn.ac.za
Website: www.ukznpress.co.za

ISBN: 1-86914-096-6

Editor: Kobus Moolman
Layout and design: Rock Bottom Design
Cover picture: *Marabenta Dance* by Ezequiel Mabote
Cover design: Flying Ant Designs
         Sebastien Quevauvilliers

Printed and bound by Interpak Books, Pietermaritzburg

Dedicated to President Thabo Mbeki for preaching the message of love and peace amongst nations. For his pledge to promote gender equity and improve the lives of all South Africans.

To my family for their tolerance and for encouraging me to stand up.

Acknowledgements

'Intaba Zebhukazana'; 'I'm A Man'; 'In Memoriam Sizwe Kondile'; 'The Question'; 'Strange Things'; 'Next Time Use a Rope'; and 'Ukuhlangana no Rhulumente' were published in *Strange Things* (Snailpress, 1994). 'Being Human'; 'The Same Procession'; 'Credence'; 'He Came Down the Street'; and 'Impassable Bridge' were published in *When Rains Come* (Carapace Poets, 2000).

Thanks to Kobus Moolman and Robert Berold for their critical contributions.

Contents

Closing Ceremonies

I can't believe this!
Come and see!
My wife said.
A figure catwalked up the road
With unseeing eyes,
An escaping corpse,
A skeleton dressed
For closing ceremonies.

It's him alright
His time is up,
I said.

He used to be so strong
Look at him now
I could hardly recognise him,
She said.

We watched the road-show,
A disturbing sight
That left a lingering feeling.
He spoke to no-one
As he ambled,
Now and then flashing his teeth
Like a snarling beast
As he greeted passersby.
He wants to see his friends
Before the bell rings,
I said.

A few weeks later
We saw a hearse at his home.

Intaba Zebhukazana

(The Hogsback Mountain)

The steep mountains of Katberg
Locked with the Hogsback
With the Winterberg
Form Lushington basin
Fearfully high to strangers
And equally high to travellers
Yet too shy in rainy months
Always hiding in the fog.
On wintry days sleeping under snow
A haven for a thousand hogs
Wealth of the mountain tribe
Flora and petra*
Pride of nature's finger
Carved for tiny souls
A freedom from mankind.

I long for berries
Wild fruit and game
I miss cliffs and waterfalls
Spewing fury in white rage
That petrified me as a child
Mysteries of nature
Springs and streams
No drought could tame,
Their water is nostalgic.
I yearn for stock and crops
Produce of the peasants
The generous soil
A pleasure to the tiller.
I miss the vulture's plea
Keen to caress a carcass
Of a horse that has served its master.

Everywhere I went strange looks followed
Names of childhood friends
Had never been heard
Where their homes stood
Now tall trees grow
And where I was born
A big dam smiles,
It has swallowed the past.
I wanted to scream
Of course they'd whisper
'I told you! He's mad!'
For answers I looked at the mountain
With tiny footprints
They were threateningly huge.

Could those baboons and buck
Which we once hunted
Recognise me for old time's sake?
I felt thirsty but springs were dry
Willows oaks and stones
Had they lost their special names?
I stayed away from you
Land of our forefathers,
But you keep pulling me
Like a spell.

---

* Rock formations

3

Being Human

In my life
I planted seeds and seedlings
Which had brief appearances.

Though very few
I also planted trees,
Whose shade now cancels my shadow
And whose height dwarfs my ego.

Raising young ones is lovelier
And toughest by far.
Their easy laughter
Puts a spark in my life,
But each time they break
It kills a part of me.

I'm A Man

We spent the night drumming and dancing
Singing songs of courage.
Was it not the last
We would be together?
When the ripening period comes
We catapult
Into the waiting world
Like the seed of dry pods.

The crunching frost
Under my unshod feet
The biting breeze
Of that winter's dawn
Skinning my naked body
Menacing sticks and threatening words
Before I was forced
To break the icy stream
Was it a sort of vendetta?
Numb in body and soul
I cursed through chattering teeth
Like a caged beast
And defied the cutman's stiletto
That left a crimson ring
Round my shrunken stick of manhood
Where the stigma was
And I declared the divine words
Of the ultimate stage,
'I'm a man!'

The Abduction

I stood on the banks of the Tyhume
Awed by moans of that furious deluge
Grabbing and uprooting debris
Dragging it down its snaky bends,
A dragon disturbed in its slumber
Laying destruction in its wake.

A young woman across
Was negotiating for her passage
With a row of thirsty stones,
To come over to my side.

In an instant
Its wet hands snatched her by the legs
Muffled her screams and dragged her underneath
And were it not for yells that invaded my ears
She would have vanished
With the hurtling rubbish.

It dragged her headlong
Bobbing and flipping
Trying to grab
Anything in reach of her fingers.
But the trees standing on the banks
Like a guard of honour
Were washing their hands.
The Tyhume was abducting her
To appease its angry gods.
How I plunged into the stream

Defied the raging beast
The entangling arms of the octopus,
Escapes my tongue.

I wrestled its muscular arms
Kicking and slapping
To unstrap the choking victim
Who seemed even stronger
Than the Tyhume river,
As she strangled and bundled me
To be an offering in her place.

All the while reciting a requiem,
*Ndibambe, ndibambe, ndibambe!**
In a liquid dance.

* Hold me, hold me, hold me!

Winning Nation

Our children must be champion liars and connivers
The type that will make the devil cringe
They must learn skills in corruption
The government cannot do it alone
The world must know that we've arrived
Groomed to beat any nation.

We should not forget to make them
The nimblest of all thieves
The type that will make the devil sob
Our country needs world champions
Who will parade our flag with pride
We must employ unrepentant rapists
The type that will make the devil flee.

Finally, we must send them to America
To learn deceit and manipulation
They have world champions there
The type that makes the devil restless
Ask Congo and Iraq
The United Nations can testify.

State of Emergency

An emergency
Dragged me out of the house
       that morning
To visit another suburb.
I saw the army patrolling the veld
But I didn't know
That it was to seal off our township.
I left the main road,
Took a short cut through the cordon
To my destination.
       Stop that car! Stop it!
One of them shouted
And I was stopped.
       En waar gaan jy nou?[1]
Nie ver nie,[2]
Net om die hoek, Sersant.[3]
       Jy kan nie.[4]
       Jy moet by die roadblock deur ry.[5]
There's no need for that, sir.
Otherwise I'll be late.
I got out of the car and ran.
Skiet hom! Hy moet nie weg gaan nie![6]
Skiet hom![7]
The same voice sounded
and I looked back.
They were on their knees aiming at me,
But I ignored them.
What were they worried about?
I was going to come back
And satisfy their curiosity.

There was no shooting
And I ran up the street
To my destination.
When I came back they were still waiting

On their feet
Watching me
Through their rifles.
I was running towards them
Like a child into the outstretched arms
Of his father.
I wanted to show them my honesty.
But the nozzle of a rifle punctured my zeal.
> *Why didn't you stop when we ordered you?*
> *Do you know that you almost got killed?*
I was going to come back, Sergeant.
My message was urgent
And I was going just round the corner.
> *Jy praat kak nou!*[8]
> *Maak seker hy ry terug na die roadblock!*[9]
He commanded his subordinates
But that's too far, Sergeant,
Surely you can search my car here
Or should I search it for you?
> *Do as I tell you, now!*
> *Do you think we've come for a circus here?*
No, sir! You've come to kill us.
> *Koporaal! Stuur hierdie vuilgoed na die roadblock.*[10]
> *Ek is gatvol!*[11]

1. And where are you going now?
2. Not far,
3. Just round the corner, Sergeant.
4. You can't.
5. You must drive through the roadblock.
6. Shoot him! He mustn't get away!
7. Shoot him!
8. You're talking crap now!
9. Make sure he drives back to the roadblock!
10. Corporal! Send this piece of rubbish to the roadblock.
11. I am fed up!

Those Who Hold the World

Those who hold the world
In the palm of their hands
Fold it like a handkerchief.
They wring, twist and shake it
Like a dirty rag
To rid it of burrs
And hurt those on the fringes.

In Memoriam Sizwe Kondile

*Sizwe Kondile was kidnapped from Lesotho by the state security forces.
He was detained and tortured at Jeffrey's Bay. He was injected with
poison and then taken, unconscious, to Nkomati where he was shot
and incinerated while his killers had a braai.*

They yanked him from the phone
With the skill of wolves
Bundled and brought nearer home
To tear his soul.
His cries filled the motherland
And we gasped appalled,
'Shall we see him again?
When will they stop?'
He was so close
Yet we didn't know.

With needles of death
They punctured his life,
At Nkomati signed for the soul.
A gun salute
Sealed the deal with the devil.

They were laughing
When they set him ablaze
Making an offering to gods.
They were dancing
While they braaied alongside
Starting the fire from his ashes
Eating and drinking with joy
A satanic communion
To dare God.
They ate him
And left no bone
That we may bury
That we may bury.

Time Has Come

Time has come for me
To bare the mystery of the pyramids.

It is time to reroute
The frolicking river from downstream.
It is time to teach the West
That greatness is not measured
By the number of graves
Their weapons pile.

It is not the time
To choose an ideal tree
From which to hang my lamp.

The Same Procession

He looked up the street
And saw a procession.

Scratching his beard
He went inside the house
For a camera.

When he came out
And focussed on the target,
Through the eye of the camera

He saw the same procession.

The Roadblock

I came to a roadblock
At the entrance of the township
The tired sun had already retired
Behind faraway horizons.
A Chacklas* stopped me and commanded
Get out!
We're going to search the car!
Where's your driver's licence?
I handed him my document
Muzzled by surging anger
Because that group excelled in breaking souls.
He paged through the ID.
His female colleague approached
And suddenly exploded:
Is it you?
Didn't you know that we would meet one day
When you insulted us?
(I've never seen this one,
I said to myself)
I'm talking to you
You motherfucker!
She said this advancing
Eyes reflecting madness.
(The only person ever to call me that
landed in hospital.)
My anger dissipated
Overtaken by fear
Because I knew that
It costs slight fuel
To provoke high flames.
My sister, you're mistaken,
We've not met before.

You call me your sister now?
You motherfucker!
She tried to grab her friend's shotgun
Who refused, but tried to calm her down,
And she became more deranged.
Some of her colleagues came closer
To witness the murder, nonchalantly.
Then I knew that my turn had come.
She hurried to a nearby armoured truck.
Her colleague handed back my ID
And quietly said,
Get in your car!
The woman came back
And gave her shotgun one violent massage.
Fright paralysed my tongue;
So she's going to kill me
'In self-defence'
So that my brains decorate
The steering wheel,
I told myself.
The guy shielded me with his back
Arms stretched out
Like a farmer cornering a pig.
He pleaded with her
Not to puncture my life.
He said, calmly,
Start the car and go.
Very gently I pulled away,
Ears tuned for that deafening sound.

---

* During the 1980s, when South Africa's struggle for liberation was at its peak, the Nationalist Government recruited blacks to beef up its over-stretched police force. These recruits were given crash courses and were referred to as Kits Konstabels ('Instant Constables'). They were notorious for their brutality. Communities called them 'Chacklas' (from 'AmaTshaka' – 'People of Tshaka'), a term which they hated with passion.

Election Choir

Tenor: Countrymen!
            Elect me your president
            And you'll be masters
            In the art of grovelling.

Alto: Make me your president
            And I'll open for you
            The locked gates
            To gardens of madness.

Soprano: I'll make this country
            A paradise for high-flying birds
            And a desert for lizards
            If you elect me your president.

Bass: I pledge tentacled thieves
            To guard your welfare
            Rapists with hearts of steel
            To sing you lullabies
            And murderers
            Laughing with bloody teeth
            To watch over you while you sleep
            If I'm your president.

Chorus: Countrymen!
            Elect me your president
            And you'll be Olympic Champions
            In chasing your tails.

Credence

It is not these scented fragile flowers
Boastful but with a brief passage.
Nor these bright shiny leaves
Which will soon succumb
Frustrated by winter.

Nor these branches
Fanning elegantly
In all directions,
Whose boughs will be withered by seasons.

But the sombre unseen roots
That afford life to this plant.

The Question

People say children are alike
It confounds me
How much they change with time.
When we were young
We didn't ask
Why people threw stones
Into the river
Before they crossed in the evening;
Why we were warned
Never to point a finger
At the sky.
We never asked why elders panicked
When a tree-dassie
Sauntered into the yard
Or a hen crowed.
We didn't ask
Why hunters turned for home
If a snake or leguaan
Crossed their path;
Why peasants refrained
From ploughing
Or digging holes
Till a dead person was buried.

Now that I'm a parent
Children ask
Why I bury the carcass
Of an animal struck by lightning.
They ask why I worry

When a swarm of bees
Make a hive at my door;
Why I'm troubled
If an owl
Hoots from the roof of my house.

Soon they'll tell me
Why women confront the mother
If the infant refuses her breast
But accepts that of a stranger.

Is it because they are asking
That this world is changing?
Or is the world changing
Because they are asking?

The Thirst

When the day tucked in
Her blanket of heat
I took off
With my sick little brother.

Before we left
They stressed it upon us
That if along the way
We took no lengthy rest
We would catch the train
Leaving the station at dusk.

The stubborn sun
Glaring overland
Had sucked all moisture
And the few streams
That we came across
Had not known water for many moons,
And our energy was dying.

I kept murmuring to myself,
Will he make it?
Won't he die on the way?
I was thirteen and scared.
Death, a patient vulture
Was escorting us.

'I'm thirsty! I need water to drink,'
My little brother said
And my heart sank.
I opened his *muti* bottle,
A concoction of aloe and other herbs,
Which a *sangoma* had prepared
To ease or delay his death.
I offered him and said,
'Here, drink little brother.'
And I watched him;
It was all that we had.

After a sip
His face turned into an ugly mask
And I took the stuff back
To calm my burning throat.
After a gulp
My face twisted into an ugly mask
My little brother laughed.
We continued with our journey.

An animal dam across the fence
Beckoned us
But drought had cracked
Even its thirsty belly
Except where hooves
Had left deep impressions,
Brown smelly liquid remained.
We looked at each other
Resignedly.

Let Us Lower Our Flag

We stopped complaining
And moaning to our children;
We stopped waiting for them
To cook our meals.

Our sons don't cling to shining ideas;
When the night spreads out
Her blanket of darkness
They peep under lifted skirts,
Wine and money their mission.
They don't live to be ancestors.

Though we try to shield them
And listen to their young voices
Still, the wolf comes.

It is a tragic season
When our offspring can't hear anymore.
It is time to lower our flag.

Times Like This

Before he died
Father should have warned me
That there would be times
When I'd feel that God had forsaken me.
Maybe he was a stranger to God.

He didn't tell me
That there would be times
When even close friends would flee from me
As if from a leper.
Maybe he forgot to.

He should have taught me
That there would be times
When even those who've known my kindness
Would dress me
In a mask of a demon.

At least he should have advised me
Where I should search
When my well of wisdom
Showed the bottom.
Maybe he was still going to tell me.

It is hard now
I'm staring at nothing
Listening to the sound of emptiness
Because I didn't know that
At my age
There would be times like this.

Strange Things

A man followed a madam
Into a house . . .

When he went home
She was at the window
Listening to his footsteps
Gazing at the township.

When her husband returned
He helped her into a chair.

They Don't Tell Me

I chose a silent rock
To sit myself upon
And mouthed my tidings.
But those who came with ears of gossip
Charged me with looking for fame
They forced me across rivers and mountains
To tell my stories
On foreign soil.
But each time I ask
They don't tell me
Why I sing best
When I suffer most.
They don't advise me what to do
When I choke from unsaid lumps of thoughts
They don't tell me
How to frustrate the wrath of cysts
That will invade my tongue
If I shut up my mouth
They think I've eaten poisonous mushrooms.
They say I'll soon tire
Of never catching my tail
That I will flip belly-up
A dying lizard in surrender.
But the wind's flapping wings
Fan my lyrics
To those who will hear.

We Won't Be Silent

Even if they plug their ears
We won't brush our words with oil,
Throw our arms up in the air,
Shaking our heads.
Those who eat prickly pears
Should first consider the consequences
Because our secrets
Though silent as thunder
Are not meant for our own ears.
We sing to embarrass
The fury of unuttered words
Fermenting in our heads.

A Lullaby for Rape Victims

If we had words
We'd pipe tongued lyrics
Soft lullabies
Into your ears
Nurse your transgressed souls
Like gentle water
Sprinkling over flowers
Whose soil has been disturbed.

We may not have been there
To soothe your sobs,
Still, the flowers must bloom
To decorate the land
Where only God's hand
Is on show
And the devil
Potbellied with evil
Has no room.

Oh My God!

In our struggle against the beast
We may have erred
In causing disorder.

Our children
Are now familiar with disorder
Estranged from respect.

Too Late

I

Let those who may
Hold the devil's hand
And learn his ways.
Maybe before I retire
To my ultimate room
I might as well help
In building the nation.
We've gone beyond the point
Of teaching our young
The word respect.

High-stationed hybrids
Blinded by Western wisdom
Laid foundations
Of alien values
And aggravated the fact
By opening floodgates.
They have bound our hands
That we may not reroute
The wave of erosion.

II

I shall not wonder
What I should do
To mould the young;
Those born empty of compassion

I will teach
To kill with tenderness.
That will be my contribution.

I shall give to rapists
Roaming without ears
Crumbs of humanity
(We've nothing left)
To show a bit of respect.
We cannot stop them anyway
From their bestial feelings.

It is too late
Too late to turn the tide.

Hearken My Children

When we come to this world
We each carry a package
For the long journey ahead.

The life of the wise is tranquil
Like the silent water of a stream
Now and then obstructed
By falls and cataracts
Yet getting stronger afterwards
Steadily swimming
Towards its destination.

Wisdom eludes those
Who use theirs lavishly
Throwing caution to the wind.
With accompanying misery
Their futile turbid ways
Are like violent waves,
Continuously
Going coming and crashing
Going coming and crashing.

Illusions

Tomorrow I'll kneel
Next to my father's grave
He must tell me why
There's scuff on my neck
Now that I've found
The woman of my life.

I'll stand over my mother's grave
She must tell me why
My woman's eyes
Burn holes in my wallet.
They must tell me
Why I hear yells of chimpanzees
When the woman of my heart
Approaches.

Mirage

The *sangoma* bellowed,
'The wrath of ancestors
Envelops your house!
Offer them a beast and beer.'

The burdened man cried to his ancestors,
'Your wrath envelops my house.
I've heeded your calls
Met with your demands;
But you've filled my child's head with madness
And my wife's forgotten her name,
She's laughing to herself.
Air howls in our stomachs.
Why is the owl still hooting on my roof?
Why are bees invading my house?
Why are ants dancing in my room?
Tell me,
Why is the reptile cuddling in my hearth?
Why do flies sing while we sleep?
Why do vicious dogs maul me in my dreams?

Tell me,
Why we never know it when you're happy?
Why you never thank my offerings?'

Time to Go

For many decades now
I've not witnessed a cow giving birth
I've not seen the newborn calf dancing a waltz
I miss the sight of an egg hatching.
I wish I could raise enough noise
From a cowhide drum
To repel a kite
Dancing in the sky.
I miss the chorus of weaverbirds
Crocheting from lazy willow trees
Over laughing currents.

I wish I could watch a bird
Watching with marbled eyes
Its chicks learning to fly.
I miss the lonely eagle's plea
From a mountaintop
I even miss the fragrance
Of orchards in spring
Cuddled in tender rays of the sun.
How I'd love to sow and observe
New life sprouting from farm fields.

It's time to go now
Before wisdom escapes my head,
Having listened to things said
Rather than done.

The Forgotten

When jelly collects
On my wrinkled knees
When the night rolls out
Her blanket of chill,
Under the milkwood tree
I'll gather the young
Tell them about those
Who were not to belong to the future,
But to be left
To remember their songs of freedom
Their untiring hands,
And felled compatriots
Beside their country's highways.

A Bad Samaritan

He came flying through the door
A lamb bleating for its mother:
   Tata! Tata! Please hurry
   Granny is dying!
Go to sleep my boy
And let her go, I said.
But he stood there
A lump of flesh.

Lulu! Lulu! Please wake up,
That woman is dying
I don't know what to do,
Her husband is in hospital!
I pleaded with my wife.
   Get the car round to her front door
   An ambulance will be too late.

She bolted to our neighbour's house.
In her morning gown.
The woman lay on her bed
Seemingly lifeless
Lulu was trying to bring her back
Using a discarded respirator.

The car is at the front
Can I get someone to drive?
   We don't have time
   Let's take her to hospital, quickly!
   Lift her by the shoulders!
She's too heavy, I can't!

Of course you can!
Get behind the shoulders,
Can't you see what we've got here?

She's pissed on my pants!
  She's gone, that's why.
  Come on, lift her up!
  And stop moaning!
But she's floppy and jelly
We won't stuff her into the car
  Shut up and get moving!

Look! She's pissed on my pants
And I stink,
Can I go and get changed?
  Start the car and let's go!

Moths

Lured by light
Spurred by self-interest
They fly from all directions
In every dimension
For best positions
Self-satisfaction,
Strangers to shame.
Their short-lived joy
Ends in misery,
A kiss of death.
They blanket the floor.

Next Time Use a Rope

He lived fatherless
For thirty-five years.
Before he was ten
His mother abandoned him
For a better life
Of vagrancy
And hallucination of meths
Turning her heart into stone
A path he later chose
For escape or success.
In his struggles to survive
He lost an eye,
And the lamp was further dimmed.

One evening they found him groaning
Like a bullfrog under a hedge
Belly taut with rattex.

I met him coming from hospital
We laughed
About his rodent appetite.
He said life was cruel
I said, 'Next time use a rope –
You won't fail.'

Two nights later
A school watchman
Found him dangling
Like a maize-cob in a hut roof.
Friends and relatives
Put him deep in a hole.

Stranger

My phone rang
In the middle of the night
A shaky voice from afar said,
'We've not met before
But I've heard of you.
Can you please, help my son
He is stranded in town?
He is there to get educated
But almost got robbed
When he got off a taxi.'
I said, Shit!

Five months later the parent phoned,
And said,
'It's me again
I phoned you early this year for help
Do you remember?
Can you please, ID my son's body
At Mount Road mortuary?
He was mugged in Central, first.
Then they found his body dangling
In his flat.'
I said, Shit!

A few days later my phone rang,
She said,
'Can you go to Home Affairs
For his death certificate?
And can you collect from his flat
All his belongings?

Finally, can you collect
An autopsy report
From the investigating officer?'
I said, Shit!

A week later she phoned and said,
'You've been so kind,
We'd like to include you in the programme
To talk about his last journey,
It would be good
To hear it from the horse's mouth.'
I said, Which journey?

Times Change

In the past
Elders forbade the young
From going near a place of death.
Now that we are parents
We take the children to funerals
To get them used to death.

It licks them.

There Will Be Signs

My fat-necked potbellied brothers
Glide in cars of the future
Marry mechanical women
With names like Computer and Jacuzzi.
They melt behind iron curtains
In dream houses with swimming pools,
The envy of white folk.
They speak a language
Which is the heart of domination
And send their children
To the best institutions
To lift them above the lot.
And I say
Soar high, brothers;
Isn't this what we fought for?

They offer us tribal bones
Brushing their words with honey
Prescribing us the past
From which they flee.
Is it right
That we should adopt
Ways of lizards
And not also learn to fly?
Is it right that we should backtrack
While the world around is changing?
They say,
Go back to your roots and stay there!

Father said that
When the snarl of caressing dawn comes
There will be signs.

Ukuhlangana no Rhulumente

(Meeting with the Government)

I remember when I was young
There were forests
Where people could not chop,
Lands where their animals
Could not graze
Kuba yayiyeka Rhulumente.
It perplexed me
That this unseen man
Could own so much
Command more respect than God.

One day over the ridge
Emerged people riding
And men of the village
Took to their heels
And vanished in a forest.
Grandpa a retired teacher
Had remained dignified
On his ancient chair near the kraal.

The party sauntered
Through our property.
With granny and children of the house
We came to sit next to him
Watched the horses
Deposit their luggage
Near the kraal.

Grandpa was a big man
But he was dwarfed by the White man
Whose stomach made him look
Like a full-term python.
They were all clad in khaki,
Shiny brown boots
With legwear
Hats like tortoise shells
Swords dangling at their sides.

I don't know what they talked with grandpa.
After they had gone
He told us
Yayingu Rhulumente.**
For many months after
People remained perturbed.

---

* It belonged to the Government
** It was the Government

Man is Dead

Man
Is always
At the forefront;
Was the first in Eden,
Trailblazing for woman.
He was first on the moon
To stage a coup against God.
He is the one who started wars,
Passion of the hidden rebel.
He was the first to die.
Now man is dead
Man is dead
Is dead
Dead.

When I'm King

The day is not yet over the mountain
And still far away
Before I too
Declare myself King.
Though I'm fiftyish
I should rule by example
By marrying a juvenile
In her prime
To resuscitate my life.
But, since I'm a commoner
People say that choice
Is child abuse and abominable.

When I become King
A sire of good stud
I will not be accused of molestation.
Lavish praises and adoration
Will be heaped on me
For sowing rare seed.

Water In a Sieve

When the state extended
Its sympathetic hand
To children
Whose fathers were hidden in the ground,
Young women flocked to graveyards
With pens and papers,
Searching for cold names.

When the government decreed
A support grant
For children of lizards,
Little girls became *boepens**
So that they too could queue
And be rewarded for lifting their skirts.

When the country waved
Its generous hand
To victims of Aids
Young women took to taverns
Then filed to hospitals to be tested
To qualify for the grant.

* Had extended stomachs

When He Ceased to Dream

When he ceased to dream,
he curled himself
like a foetus
on the bench
under the blue blanket of the sky.

The lonely moon smiled.

My Gratitude

I thank my teachers
For their eagle patience
In teaching me to fly.
I cannot forget childhood friends
Who ran and laughed with me.

I salute those comrades
Who didn't bow to gods of fortune,
Trade our burden with the gold of this land.
I pay tribute to countrymen
For reaching out to me.

I cheer our athletes
For parading this flag.
I sweep paths for those leaders
Who observed and learnt
From the shame of chameleons.

I thank the woman
Who brought me into this world.
Most importantly I thank God
For putting me in this land,
Where else would I rather be?

He Came Down the Street

He came down the street
In one hand
Holding a live chicken
By its wings
In the other
A packet of onions
And potatoes.

My Duty

I've resolved to extend my days
And equip my children with deep roots
To embarrass the storms of life.
Unless this task is achieved
I'll have failed in my duty.

I've been advised to stay a bit longer
Until I've written a poem
That will telescope the fount of my lyrics,
Having flogged the truth to such shreds
Scholars are bound to raid my grave.

I've been asked to walk a few more miles
And try to make an imprint
Because it does not help to cry
When it thunders.

I'll live a few more seasons
To raise an issue with God,
Before He rings the bell
He must roll up my sins
And explain my contractual terms.

New Proverbs

Unless the route of a root
Fulfills the purpose
A plant cannot live.

Though we dance in the sun
There are those below
Who will not know warmth.

A tree may yield in abundance
But it can never enjoy its fruit.

Many hands build a house,
But few are destined to cuddle at its hearth.

He taught his girl skills
In hide and seek.
She fell pregnant and hid the source.

Grandpa had no water tap in his house
Father had one
I have five.

Our parents never taught us
That the deepest wounds
Are caused by those
Very close.

Those in front
Did not warn those following
That words crush men's testicles.

God placed us on earth
That we may learn.
Many go back empty-headed.

The greedy
Sing our anthem loudest
Hoist the national flag highest.

He said,
Why don't you write your name on rocks?
I said, I carve it in people's hearts.

I've left my footprints on the beach a hundred times
But each time I go back to check
They have vanished.

People Change

In the past
when we came
across a corpse
we changed course
or crossed our hearts.
Today we tilt its head
prise its mouth open
to rob it of its gold-
sheathed teeth.

The Mountain

They came to me and said
Let's make offerings
To our hungry spirits.
I said,
We've outgrown our nest,
Let's soar to great heights
Where spirits dwell.

They put their lips in my ears and cried,
Child of our mother
Let's appease our angry gods!
I said,
We are born of one womb
Allow me to freeze this family name
Now that the curse has begun.

With bifocal vision
We drink, dance, pray and die,
But the mountain does not move.

Dancing in the Rain

I'm used to throwing stones
At nests high up in trees.
I'm used to convex shapes
Of the backs of our dogs.
As a child I grew up on loaves of pain
Like one marked out for this fate,
Now I'm done with hurling stones
At every nest above.
Now that there are answers
To the sweat of my brow
I let beautiful things grow.
Joy has invaded my heart
I'm a South African
And I'm dancing in the rain.

No-Amen

When the outstretched hands of the sun
Were surrendering their grip,
When the big eye in the sky
Was bidding the earth goodbye,
Villagers gathered outside their huts
And listened to No-Amen
Piping her practiced lamentation.
Her homestead, a cluster of houses,
Was tucked under the belly
Of the Hogsback Mountains
Beneath the laughing cliffs
That trumpet sound over the village,
At the feet
Of a curled-up hill
Hidden in thick bushes.

Two wives were not enough
For Ndondela,
The stud whose vigour
Made him spend nights
In different kraals
As if his was the best penis
In the whole village;
But No-Amen had grown tired
Of spending nights alone.
She would see him
Slip out of the homestead
On his escapades
Before she emerged

To stand on the overlooking hill
In the cover of bushes
To trumpet her melancholy:

Ndondela has deserted his house
He is spending the night
Wrapped in white sheets
Of his willing whore.
My husband will spend the night
Between the thighs
Of his willing whore!
The unfailing cliffs
Took up her elegy,
Music from a new organ,
Sweet words in the brimming hearts
Of certain mothers,
But some parents were worried
For our virgin ears.

One day we saw him coming down
In his outing overcoat
To lie near a secret boulder
In the shy bushes
Before the night's cloak of sins
Covered the village.
That day we didn't expect No-Amen
To address the village
On his confused promiscuity;
But she emerged all the same
And made herself comfortable

Near the boulder
For the long night ahead
When she would belch fire
Shaking the Hogsback Mountains
Leaving men ill at ease.

Ndondela has absconded again
To spend the night wrapped
In the white sheets
On Mntshakaza's farm.
He is cuddled between the thighs
Of his willing – Aah!
A fury of blows
From Ndondela's violent stick
Cut her sermon short.
The cliffs took up her wail
And telephoned it across the village
To open ears of gossip.

No Regrets

In the last days of my life
What will bob in the chambers of my heart
Are childhood memories
At the bottom of my chest
Imprints of wise words
Carved by those who blazed my way.

I'll be free of regrets,
I have sired no illegits
Whose cries will follow my footsteps,
I've shattered no souls
Whose tears will flood my final straight,
I may have failed to stall
Man's rotten morals
But my slate before God
Has no blot.

No More Flowers Left

In the past it was a tragedy
For a girl to have a child
Now it is a shame to be a virgin;
Every child suckles a child
A trophy for early parenthood.

Young Adults

Our children do not laugh
Like those of yesterday
I'm told that theirs is a better world
Of computerised games.
They don't play with homemade toys
That filled our hearts with joy.

They go to taverns
And become parents
At the age of twelve.
They meet with death
Sooner than we did.

The Betrayal

Tribal tongues are howling
To undo
What was so painfully attained
As the greedy sing
Our national anthem
With full mouths.
They shred our country's flag
And soil its legal pages.

They have forgotten to remember
Those who sacrificed their lives
Through the outrage of rivers
And ambush of maiden forests
Undivided by mountains.

Their Democracy

Heaps and heaps of graves
Are piled in Iraq
In the name of democracy.
Truth is
Western democracy
Can only stand
If its foundations
Are firmly mortared on corpses.

You Must Know

You must know, Son
That there's a time in man's life
To be turned
Into a solitary tree
Upon which birds build their nests,
Raid it for its fruit
And smudge it with droppings.

Remember, my Son
That this is the time
When seasons' storms
Will test your strength
By wrestling your boughs
To see if you have roots
Strong enough
To embarrass hurricanes.

Stand firm in the hearts
Of those who love you
And grow strong
From blows of suffering
Because the life of an upright man
Is the salt of this world.

Death of a Neighbour

There was no rain
To douse the raging flames
Work of violent arsonists,
But the cry
Of a heartbroken mother
To greet their steps.

It was too late when the jetting hoses
Of firemen hissed
To confirm the death
Behind the darkened ruins.

It was too late when the police came
To collect his tragic bones,
Yet on the next day
A wailing wind came
To fly his spirit away.

In My House

In the last days
There was a call
For a final push
On the rotting tree
So that its fall
Could echo throughout the world.

A flock of birds
Feasting on its worms
Scattered to nearby bushes.
Sadly the grounded tree
Was not incinerated
And its vermin snuggled underneath.

Then a house was built
Where the blighted tree stood
And more parasites were positioned
To descend like a wave of locusts,
Suckers who feared no shame;
All soiling their nails with dirt
As temptation invaded their heads.

Our elders conferred,
This looting is a shame
Let's frustrate it from its roots
Or hunger will not allow
The poor to rest.
This freedom is for mankind,
We must call the elders of the South!
And the SADEC[1] was born.

Human floods from the north
Were already swimming south
And once more our elders conferred,
We cannot turn the tide from downstream;
Just because we tread
Upon an open path
Does not mean that
We shall never falter;
But let us build dams on the mountains
And invest in peace
And NEPAD [2] and the AU [3] were born.
When the roof was in place
FIFA[4] nodded approval,
An answer to our sweat;
It is good,
We shall give you the World Cup!
The elders promised
That time had come
To loosen our belts
And for our dogs
To wear silky coats.

1. Southern African Development Community
2. New Partnership for African Development
3. African Union
4. The world soccer body

Honest Hearts

When I first saw her
She derailed my heart

She came like a vision
A goddess to maim virgin hearts,
Yet we were neighbours;
Where had she been hiding?

Day and night
She filled my thoughts
And my eyes watered for her,
But again
She vanished like a comet.

She surfaced after a month
And I invited her
Walking on air;
No! I'm not your type,
I'm rubbish
Don't waste your time on me
Or I'll break your heart,
She said.
Damaged,
My heart bled and choked
At her honesty.

It turned out
That she was my friend's sister.
He said to me,
It is true, she's rubbish
Keep away from her

Or she'll break your heart;
Most of the time she follows the wind.
Soon she was gone with the wind
This time for good.

Though I had been warned
That the cave was dark inside
I still wanted to go in
And see for myself.

The Journey

In the early days
I crawled into a farmer's shed
Like a reptile
For dry maize cobs
To thwart the air
Howling in my stomach.

In the last days
The wind's flapping wings
Will carry these stories away.

Impassable Bridge

I phoned for an MP
A former bosom friend.
His secretary asked,
In connection with what?

It punctured my ego,
I felt my manhood shrinking.

I said,
Give him my message
Tell him that poisonous mushrooms
Sprout under rotten logs.
If he asks for my name
Say it was an angered poet.
If you can do that for me
I'll be okay.

But she was quick to add,
And lizards don't fly
For their food
They crawl.

And hung up.